The Power of Us

Copyright © 2024 by Joshua David.

MILTON & HUGO L.L.C.

4407 Park Ave., Suite 5

Union City, NJ 07087, USA

Website: *www.miltonandhugo.com*

Hotline: 1-888-778-0033

Email: *info@miltonandhugo.com*

Ordering Information:

Quantity sales. Special discounts are granted to corporations, associations, and other organizations. For more information on these discounts, please reach out to the publisher using the contact information provided above.

Library of Congress Control Number: 2024914801

ISBN-13:   979-8-89285-228-9   [Paperback Edition]
979-8-89285-229-6   [Hardback Edition]
979-8-89285-230-2   [Digital Edition]

Rev. date: 08/19/2024

THE
POWER
OF US

JOSHUA DAVID

CONTENTS

PREFACE

From traveling and working around the world, and from falling on tremendous hardship here at home, I have gained a unique insight to our social problems and how to solve them. I have traveled to a variety of countries in the Americas and Asia, living and working in both Hawaii and Japan for about a decade each. During these times I learned each culture, and what I found on return home from these locales was a lot of unnecessary suffering. For a long time, I have intended to use these insights to help all of us live better. More recently, I have wanted to stop us from depriving *ourselves* of a better America, by relieving our polarized frustration and in-fighting that only serves to enable a government of rulers rather than servants of the public.

I have an extensive education spanning over 25 years in the fields of foreign language, performing arts, sociology, and psychology. Along with being a writer, I am a student for life, musician for life, and I shoot photography as well. As will be discussed later, I have also learned how to thrive in mental illness. With all of the time studying psychology from textbooks and practicing psychological principles learned in over a decade of clinical therapy, I have come to understand the ins and outs of the human condition well. My current course of study concerns things like cognitive psychology, quantum physics, and world religions in the quest to help develop a more scientific understanding of human consciousness. I hope you will find these insights in the following sections useful here as well.

My education did not just occur in the comfort of my home and in college classrooms, but also on the streets. Despite being labeled "smart" by many, and most likely because of it, I have been down the many roads of suffering described in this book. All of my hardships, however tragic, were a wake-up call and an education entirely on their own. Through all of it, I learned who I truly am, more of what it means to be human, what our challenges are, and how to get out of these challenges with what is available to us. It is my intent here to make all of this information available to you, so that we can all benefit from what I will describe as an "us" society.

It is my sincere hope that you will not only find a more compassionate and updated viewpoint on the human condition shared by all of us, but that you will also find my writing entertaining to read, enjoy fresh and bold statements, and consider some imaginative solutions to some of our most pervasive and controversial problems in American society. I have noticed that these problems not only permeate our society, but most other societies around the world as well. I know why we are struggling, and I sincerely hope to affect change here. First at home, as a model for other nations to follow; this, in order to reclaim America's place as a cultural leader on the world stage. We have always been a country of innovative solutions to common problems, and the will-power and manpower to make positive change a reality, and I would like to see this re-realized again in my lifetime.

In the authoring of this book, I have met with many professionals and passers by that have identified the need for change in all of these areas. Upon the disclosure of the insights in this book, I have received so many compliments and encouraging words that I am certain of an urgent need for the shifts described in this book. I humbly thank each and every one of them for their insights and positive feedback. The people have spoken, and after reading, I sincerely hope that you will as well. Change doesn't take a long time and hard work, deciding to make the change is the most time and energy consuming part. Once a conviction is reached to make the change, the rest begins to fall into place. With God's help and His hand of Providence, all things are possible, especially for those who work diligently to these ends.

Thank you so much for reading and I hope you decide to pass the book along or encourage others to buy a copy as well. Most of all, *enjoy*!

Yours Truly,

Joshua David

SECTION

1

INTRODUCTION TO US

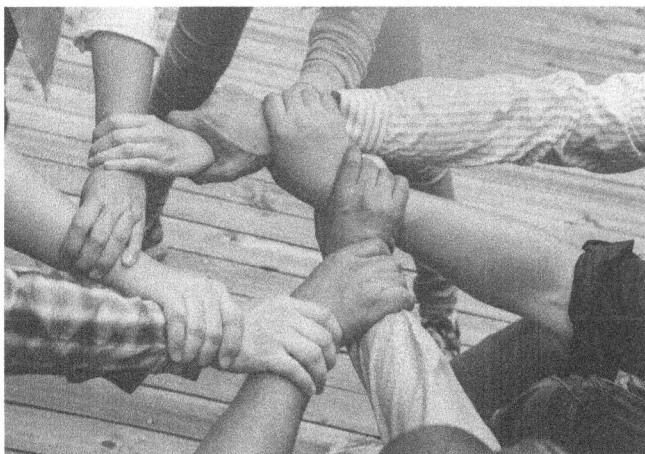

This book on "The Power of Us" started as a differential analysis of the already widely publicized "Think 'we,' not 'me~!'" movements in mental health. I saw them as insidious; inherently divisive in nature, while being sold as inclusivity. I saw that this way of thinking, however touted as being inclusive, and thus non-discriminatory, was actually the inverse. They weren't defeating stigma, they were encouraging it. All of these "we" movements that I saw that claimed to be contributing to inclusivity and recognition, were only contributing to *exclusive* recognition and perpetuating pre-existing divisive dichotomies through simple re-labeling; "normal" and "abnormal," with "typical" and "divergent."

However, during the first drafts of this book, it became apparent that I had a more broadly applicable idea that was not just limited to mental health and human development. I decided to rename the book from "Mental Diversity" to "The Power of Us" at this time. I developed it into a work that serves as a call to awareness for *actual* inclusivity and unity. It has morphed into a cry for us to stop shooting ourselves in the foot by becoming the bully we are trying to fight. In our attempts to over power or compete with the various rivals of stigma and discrimination, and lacking better insight, we only overcompensated and started fighting *ourselves*. A way out of what seemed like a cycle of creating one problem to replace another; simply relabeling each side of an old dichotomy with a newer, seemingly smart, scientific nomenclature, was to change the viewpoint of the analysis of the problems. This is to shift the focus not from "me" to "we," but further on to "us."

The Power of Us has become an advice for us to step *over*, *around*, or even stand *side by side*, *with* these problems and adversaries both internal and external; and in so doing, we stop wasting our time and emotional energy on competition and confrontation. By stopping this struggle and in-fighting, we can better focus our already limited attention to the *actual* problems, and utilize greater stamina in our more calculable and deliberate, and thus effective action on our societal crises together. Simply put, *The Power of Us* is an "us" movement, not a "we" one.

THE POWER OF US IS AN "US" MOVEMENT

The core spirit of *The Power of Us* is to shift our "we" mentality to an "us" mentality for *truly* inclusive unity. It acknowledges the logical absurdity of the many works that have said, "We must think 'we,' not 'me~!'" *The Power of Us* points out that if *we* are to move toward something new, it is a moot task to ask that "we" move to "we." It just isn't actionable. *We* need to be moving from "me," from the "they and I" of "we," and onto "we and them" of "*us;*" "we" *can* move to "us," but not "we." If *inclusion* is in fact what we are aiming to do, if solutions that benefit all of us are what we are aiming to draw up, then we need to re-frame our problems in this "*all* of us" way. It is an over-literal distinction, but it's a critical one.

"We"-thinking movements as a whole, have fallen short of their intended effect. Currently, all of our many *diversified*, not diverse, enclaves we currently identify ourselves with, have been produced by "we"-thinking. "Us," means "we" *plus* "them." "Us"-thinking is *actually* inclusive, not only by being inclusive to excluded groups, but also by being inclusive to the majority that is all others in the larger group as well. The problem with "we" thinking is that it inherently needs an outside listener to function. Someone is always exclusive, and thus someone is always being excluded. This is the simple, yet hard to recognize distinction that makes "us" *in*clusive, and "we" *ex*clusive. "We" infers a "they," and so we unwittingly use this divisive term instead of the actually unifying term "us," just because it rolls off the tongue better, "Think we, not me~!"

"*They*," must also be present in "we" for "we" to work as advertised, if moving from "me" to "we" is what we were intending to do in the first place. "Us" is inherently *unifying*, and "we," although similar, is inherently *divisive* because when "we" stand for anything, it implies separation from someone else, as in "*We* The People." "We The People," *is* inclusive, but only to us in America. It requires an outside listener for it to make sense, and this was its intended use in this situation. "We," the *Citizens of The United States of America*, declare "x," "y," and "z" *to* the King of England, and the world at large." "Here *we* stand." Beautiful!

"We," is generated when *separating* "us" from "them;" and this was a good thing for us in America. We only use "we" when describing ourselves to an outside party. I, the author of this book, refer to "us" as "we" when writing, because I'm writing to *you*, my reader. We can only identify with our infinitely diverse humanity, by using "us." "You," and "I," *and* "They," *all,* belong to the unified and all-inclusive group that is "us." "Us," is therefore the *only* logic that we can utilize in order to be *equally* inclusive to *all* of us, and not only inclusive to particular "we"-groups. "We"-groups unwittingly promote division and not unity, by promoting only the diversity of select groups of individuals within our *collective* society. In doing so, we stand out against one another and against the majority that is not of said exclusive group, a majority that also comprises all other minority groups.

A unifying movement for "us," like *The Power of Us*, has a greater chance for actual realization and broad implementation than inherently *exclusive*, "we"-movements. This is because "us" is not exclusionary, but inclusionary by default; that in order to solve the problems of each social crisis, we must be working together and working from a place of "all of us" for any real change to take place. "Us" is also more defensible because even if some choose not to identify with "us," they go over there with the others that are *not* "us;" creating a "them." Then, having partitioned themselves in solidarity of their disagreement with us, we can direct our efforts more efficiently to help them understand us, and bring them back into the fold. "Us" inherently enables the process of resolving disagreements quickly and amicably, because thinking in terms of "us" makes us more compassionate to others that don't identify with us.

The Power of Us can be thought of as being about asking better questions. Not "what's wrong," but "what's good?" Not "what's special," but "why is it special?" It is an awareness of the complexity and uniqueness of all of our individual experiences of reality, our persons, our personalities, and our plights. It does so by wearing different goggles that focus on the diversity of the holistic *whole* of humanity, and not by specializing our diversity, in order to *diversify* our population. Through this diversification touted as inclusion, our society has become groups of individual trees, isolated from one another in a parking lot. *The Power of Us* is built upon the logical, and moral idea that we should not stop at seeking understanding and celebrating differences, but also recognize how these differences are all differences within a *single human race* of one united, American public. This book asks us to benefit from the awe-inspiring diversity of *all* of our individualized and unique, gifted human beings, collectively, from a more macro perspective, as a gestalt product of all of the various microcosms of society.

THE NUMBERS OF WHY WE NEED THE POWER OF US

- According to wikipedia.com, up to 38.01% of Americans, approximately 128,450,00 of us, make less than $30,000 a year. [1] This is a result of the "we"-thinking economics that we currently practice that will be discussed later.

- Estimates vary, but up to ⅓ of the 338.29 million total American citizens, both youth *and* adults, suffer some form of bullying every year. If you drive a car, you know this number is most likely much higher. Well over 101,486,957 of us. [2] [3] This is the product of a disastrous tag-team between the media and us, our inability to draw boundaries, a government that tells us what to do instead of the other way around, and some logical fallacies that we will discuss later.

- According to the Substance Abuse and Mental Health Services Administration (SAMHSA,) 21.9% of the total population, 61.2 million of us, reported having used at least one illicit drug over the year in 2020. [5] It's not just the War on Drugs that is at fault, but the way we use drugs and think about them, which we will discuss later.

- According to the National Institute for Mental Health (NIMH,) in 2021, over 1 in 5 of us struggled with some form of mental health diagnosis, some 58,700,000 of us. [4] A sad number considering that we currently view mental health as a disease issue and not one of possibility.

- Although not a complete count, the National Department of Housing and Urban Development (HUD,) counted 582,500 of us as homelessness in 2022. [6] This number is likely much higher as there are just not enough reliable counting methods due to privacy and logistical issues. Again, this ties into the aforementioned as we will discuss.

- According to The Department of Justice (DOJ,) 1,230,100 were incarcerated in prison in 2022. The total number of incarcerated individuals exceeds 2,000,000 when considering prisons and jails. [7] [8] As we will see, all of the aforementioned crises contribute to this.

- According to the Centers for Disease Control (CDC,) 48,000 of us committed suicide in 2021. [9]... mostly as a result of all of the above.

As we can see, there are no small number of us afflicted by the social maladies of poverty, bullying, drug abuse, mental health, homelessness, mass incarceration, and the suicides that all of these contribute to. As we will learn, these are not isolated "they" issues. These are issues that affect *all* of us either directly or indirectly. The formula for change laid out in this book seeks to ameliorate all of these issues with simple changes of heart and some imaginative models for change that will be discussed in the last section. As we will see, change will inevitably start within our own hearts and minds, but once this is accomplished, actuation of any plans resembling each at the end of this book will be easier. This will not only bring tangible change to these issues individually, but also an entire host of secondary benefits that will compound all of these positive changes as well.

THE BENEFITS OF BEING US

The Power of Us is the seed of a beneficial idea that will grow swiftly in all of the above-mentioned areas, including advancements in economics, education, employment, and public health and safety. It could even grow to upgrade technology sectors. The benefits of this "us"-philosophy are manifold:

- A more unified public.

- A more informed human understanding.

- A better awareness of who we are individually.

- Amelioration of poverty and greed for *all*, rich or poor.

- A less bullying society.

- A decline in drug use and addiction.

- Less stigma in mental health with better mental healthcare.

- The end of homelessness as we know it.

- Lower incarceration rates.

- Safer streets for all.

- A sharp decline in deaths associated with all of the aforementioned social maladies, including suicide.

- Enhanced public health.

- Increase our GDP by more than tens of billions of dollars *annually* as an end result. The actual figure, including all secondary and societal benefits is truly *incalculable*.

- A better overall quality of life for all.

With so many benefits, it must be clear why we must take decisive action on this philosophy and practice of the 'us'-thinking of *The Power of Us*. It will bring us to an awareness that becomes the most effective way to fix all of the otherwise "impossible to solve," problems in our society, starting by identifying with "us." The rest is just learning more about what is making us and our society sick, learning some techniques, and practicing these techniques. Through this education and self-improvement, we will realize all of the cornucopia of benefits that are the vision of *The Power of Us*.

2

OUR SOCIETY IS SICK

We can change from "we" to "us" by first understanding that our society is sick because of our dichotomous and catastrophizing "we versus them"-thinking, and our diversifying "we, and we, and we over here"-thinking. We must also realize that by dichotomizing and catastrophizing social issues, our current efforts for healing are being rendered ineffective. The truth is that healing efforts are *not* doing well, and although there are pockets of light spread throughout, looking at the numbers above, we still are doing terrible. As already outlined above, there is a stepwise pattern that is formed in this interlocking and reciprocating system of deconstruction of the human character that is poverty, bullying, drug abuse, mental health challenge, homelessness, incarceration, and on to death. Indeed, it is a slippery slope, but it is a real one! This system of deconstruction doesn't need to start with being poor, but can happen to anyone, and entry onto this conveyor belt of death can happen during a single episode of any of these conditions at any time, during anyone's lifetime.

One can begin their journey into this unrelenting rotisserie of social sickness from any of the above entry points of this syndrome of symptoms that is noted above. More terrifying is that, once on this conveyor belt, it only gets more and more difficult to escape with time. For instance, we can be bullied at school, end up in mental health counseling, experiment with drugs, and become incarcerated from committing a crime as a result of drug use. The incarceration then serves to keep us locked into this system of suffering from which we may never fully recover. The pattern is not necessarily step-wise either, but we can jump around in it. For example, we lose our job and become homeless, there, in poverty and loneliness, we become addicted to drugs, are then bullied on the streets because of unpaid tabs on the drug bill, and committ suicide in hopelessness from being beat up on the streets.

Each one of these stories can be ongoing and not end in death, but reciprocate back into the beginning and repeat, and repeat, and repeat. Repetition is a mechanism for going insane, and this is how these problems become chronic. This list of social ills and conditions can run forward or backwards, jump around, heighten the probability of acquiring yet another condition, and can be thought of as a spectrum of severity for a single malady.

This syndrome of social maladies is reinforced in feedback loops, and so it is both caused by, and feeds back into all of the above noted social symptom states within it. The severity of the sickness is compounded by many social factors like stigma and narcissism from normalism in the mainstream, "non-affected" population; mismanagement of social support systems by often times nepotistic, *for-profit*-"non-profit organizations;" social stigmas concerning all of these individual conditions; and xenophobic fear of the unknown concerning one another. These are all just some of the factors that contribute to this social disease. All important to note is that, *all* of us are affected by this revolving door of social malady. There is not one person on the planet unaffected by these problems, here or far abroad.

We will believe that we are indeed affected next time we watch the news, go to a low-wage job, get needlessly honked at on our way to work, use drugs or drink to stave off the humiliation or anger, take our daily psychiatric medication, step over a debilitated homeless person on the sidewalk on our way to work, or are even scratching our head at work because of a problem that we just can't rectify. Some of our best and brightest end up impoverished, bullied, addicted, deemed "crazy," excommunicated, incarcerated, and/or will commit suicide as a result. Next time we feel lonely or frustrated, we should pause for a moment to consider if that one person that could be changing our lives or the lives of others could be currently struggling with one or more of these issues. As we have seen, the numbers certainly indicate that this is a real possibility, with many of us experiencing any one of these conditions at any given time.

Our society is sick with these problems and we are not healing from them because of the "we"-thinking approach that we have been administering during the past several decades. As we will see, simply changing the perspective from "we" to "us" will have miraculous results. Combined with using the models at the end of the book as launchpads for innovation in these areas, the end-result will be exponentially reinforced. As we have seen, all of these noted ailments in our society are reciprocal and interconnected. They are not stand-alone problems. So taking action on any one of these will show a direct or indirect benefit to all of the other areas as well. It is all one problem, and we can solve it like a *kujenga* puzzle, one block at a time until all topple, each push making the total syndrome more and more unstable than the last. It is clear what the problem is and what the benefits are to taking immediate action, so let's prepare for action by diving into some of the causes of all of this chaos in society.

In this section, we will begin our journey for change into an "us"- society by pointing out some major psychological misconceptions that we all can notice within ourselves. Like most problems in our personal lives, the crux of the problem lay within ourselves. This is why the axiom, "be the change that you want to see in the world" works. By starting to affect change by starting with ourselves, although seemingly small by comparison, we see immediate results. Not only are the results immediate, but the more we practice and internalize these principles, the more often the benefits happen, and the greater the benefits will be. Positivity in the world moves around the same way that suffering does; like a boomerang and with a butterfly effect that is infectious and generates change all over the map in places unforeseeable. Let's start with a major cause and reinforcer of this rotisserie of broiling the human spirit, normalism.

A NORMALIST SOCIETY

As humans, we have evolved a culture that is too concerned, over-reliant on being "normal." However convenient an approximate measure of a median it is, this strong and engrained attachment to "normal," and the comparisons that we make based on it, are what we will see are *arbitrary,* and counterintuitively *detrimental* to society. Although the concept of "normal" is something that can be used to approximate something like blood pressure or body temperature, to a large degree it is fatally misappropriated when thinking about the general biological, psychological, socio-economic, or moral health of a constantly evolving human condition and human being.

Humans are not rigid and precise, steel and silicon robots, we are diverse and dynamic, organic living creatures. For constantly evolving, dynamic and diverse humans, even something as measurable as blood pressure and body temperature do not have an absolute "normal" value. A lesser known medical truth is that all health metrics are unique to the individual and change according to the patient's ever-changing and relevant homeostasis, the balance point of the system of our individual bodies. Sure, there are "nominal values" but these values are any number of values within a "(generally) acceptable" range, as seen on any lab work we will do.

Some of us will have a completely "normal" and "acceptable" blood pressure that falls out of this range depending on who we are and what our body's genetic makeup and current homeostasis is, such as a trained athlete. In this way, the whole of our bodies continually adapt and evolve to perpetually changing internal and external conditions. There is no "normal" human biologically, and as we will see soon, there is simply no "normal" human, period. This is especially true in the case of personality, the way we think, and the way that we perceive reality. "Normal" is an utter fallacy and as we have seen, oftentimes a fatal error.

In the case of psychological normalcy, a good example are the inherently stigmatizing "we"-labels of "neurotypical" and "neurodivergent" currently in use in a variety of anti-stigma movements in mental health. These labels are the exact "we"-labels that are advertised as inclusivity, but are actually *exclusivity*, and are thus inherently divisive. Furthermore, because these labels discriminate protected classes, but in an exclusive way, however commonplace, they could also be argued as unethical. To not discriminate and be inclusive, is to treat all persons equally, as human beings first and foremost.

Those with mental health diagnoses, or even those that we feel are different from ourselves in personality and thinking, are too often compared to this inherently divisive, and, as we have seen, a sometimes fatal "normal," "typical," "abnormal," or "divergent." In "us"-thinking paradigms, the latter actually *does* exist, and is the true default; "all are divergent," not "all should be normal," as "normal" does not actually exist. We are *all* divergent. Have we ever met someone that is as "normal" as we are?

From our self-serving and inaccurate concept of "normal" are born intentionally divisive and stigmatizing, derogatory words and epithets. This labeling and name calling can exacerbate any mental health symptoms that one may be experiencing. In essence, by using "normal" to define our mainstream selves, and by expecting all to conform, *we* are making those with mental health diagnosis worse by adding an element of exclusion to their condition. Diagnosing them as if their difference is a disease *causes* insanity, and it is further insulting because the diagnosed also want to consider themselves "normal," or "good enough" as we deem ourselves to be. In essence, we are being deemed "*ab*normal," or "deficient," and "disordered," by others that actually suffer from a delusion that they are somehow "normal," or "typical;" that "normal" is better, when, as we will see, nothing could be further from the truth.

We not only harm others with normalist thinking and memes, but we *all*, "typical" or "divergent" can become falsely confident by a kind of Dunning-Kreuger effect of feeling more mentally "normal" or mentally "special" than we actually are. Even if we are extraordinary, it kills talent to get a big head over it. Even if we are "normal," it contradicts the label to get a big head over it. These pathologizing assertions of one's "craziness," "disorders," "deficiencies," "abnormalcy," and "normal, everyday"-ness can drive us to a false sense of superiority or inferiority from a sense that we are "normal," that we are more "special" than others, or that others are less or more "normal" than we are.

"Normal" exists, but remains relative and is not absolute. Proof of this can be found in the fact that "normalcy" fits itself to the environment and thus has no frim definition across localities. Is what's customary in The United States also "normal" and customary in Japan? Is it customary for all Americans to take off their shoes when entering the home, as it is almost "normal," and compulsory in Japan? Everyone is different in this case here in the US, and this is a great model for how to approach the differences of others no matter what the difference is, especially because this is America, a land of free and tolerant adults. Here, ways of life should have never become compulsory or knit-picky of "appropriate" and "inappropriate." What's "appropriate" and "normal" for one person does not need to be the same for everyone, this is what has been beautiful about our country. This is one thing that even Japanese have envied about American life; is that we have traditionally had broader freedom about what is OK and not OK for the individual. This is freedom. "Normal" can be a meme of fascism.

We have looked at some brief descriptions from biological, psychological, and social perspectives on how normalist, "we" thinking; "*we* are 'normal,' they are not," is a fallacy. What can we do about it? What are we to use in its place? What makes non-normalcy, divergency, superior? Let's explore these questions here.

We can change normalist thinking by using the power of "us"-thinking. When we change the "normal" of "we" to an "us"-thinking, "*diversity* is normal," "*all* people are divergent," "the same humans all do it differently," "there's no accounting for taste," great things start to happen. In the following chapter on human cognition, we will see that all of us are essentially living in our own personal hallucinations. At first this may seem scary, but it is anything but once we see the beauty of it. Accepting that there is no static, "normal" person, and that we are *all* "divergent" from one another, is the only one true way of being accepting of others and considering oneself special in a healthy regard. Let's begin to inspire this kind of thinking.

We will see that because of the immense complexity of the way the human mind is set up and utilized individually, that there is a great freedom for all of us to think however we want, and that we should always reserve the right to do so. In the same way as noted with the medical idea of "normal" blood pressure, "divergency," not "abnormality" will replace an otherwise worried athlete's trepidation that their blood pressure is so much lower than others, with a healthy respect for themselves. Seeing that they were able to train their heart to such a level that their blood pressure is much lower than the commonly accepted "normal" blood pressure; and that this is an extraordinary accomplishment and not a sign of disease, the athlete doesn't treat their blood pressure unnecessarily and ends up healthier and happier for it. Divergency works in this way, normalism does not.

UNDERSTANDING THE DIVERSITY OF THE HUMAN CONDITION

Let's begin with understanding the diversity of the human consciousness, and understanding how inaccurate normalist judgmentalism is. This brief and up-to-date overview of human consciousness is the second keystone to being more compassionate and understanding of others different from ourselves. Knowing that all are more different than we can possibly imagine opens up the heart to acceptance or tolerance, and allows for us to be *better* judges than we currently are. If we're going to judge regardless, we ought to do it well.

Over the past decade, it has been increasingly accepted in various fields of psychology that our brains literally hallucinate our own reality. That each one of us is creating a kind of stained glass mosaic of objective reality that has brighter and larger plates of glass, with differing colors, and obscured by the lead lines; all parameters and designs being dramatically unique to each individual. It is definitely a stretch of the imagination for any of us to try to conceptualize that all of us are seeing different versions of reality all of the time, yet, this *is* reality. This calls into question how we perceive others, how others perceive us, or if our actions or words are decoded properly and in line with our intentions as we communicate with others. It is not just the individual kaleidoscope of what we see, but where we see it from; and this occurs with all of our, up to twenty-eight different senses beyond just sight, smell, hearing, taste, and touch. All of which have their own stained glass mosaic evolving individually and being perceived simultaneously.

As chaotic as this may seem, it is actually a healthy self-doubt to have that leads to us asking questions of one another instead of making assumptions about others, and also falsely assuming that others know how we feel without speaking up. We are literally hallucinating our own individual reality, and there is no way to know what others are thinking, or for others to know what we are thinking unless we ask and tell. For as long as our consciousness remains this way, it is absolutely scientifically proven that we cannot actually know what "objective reality" is, objectively.

This modern model of human consciousness underscores the fact that there is no such thing as an assumption of "normal" or a "common reality" at the individual level as we have already discussed. There is therefore no such thing as an objectively "normal" person. Along with being about the robust fortification of our innate dignity and human rights, *The Power of Us* is also about studying, acknowledging, celebrating, and utilizing the difference in our cognition and mentation, an awareness that is currently called "neurodiversity," but also taking into account that *all* of us are diverse. We can enjoy the benefits of the richly nuanced spectra comprising our collective consciousnesses at an individual level, and for the greater good.

COGNITION

Cognition is commonly referred to as "the process by which we acquire information from our senses and process this information." For the purposes of this book, we are going to use this same common definition. Cognition is like the hardware set up of our body's data collection through the senses, our cerebral processing engine, and thinking gearbox. There are some out there that dazzle us with intelligence. Much of what we perceive as intelligence is the beautiful way one's thought-processors are lined up and utilized for a given task. For instance, we would be deemed "smart," if we were able to use working-memory to a degree where we can remember all twenty of the items on our shopping list, add up all of the prices and tax, and know how much is owed even before the cashier scans the items. There are actually some who have no problem doing this task! This would be an example of a cognitive setup, rich in working memory potential, and proof positive that not everybody is the same; that neurodivergence can be an asset, a beautiful thing, even if it doesn't mean a diagnosis.

Yet, as apt as we may be for tabulating the cost and remembering all of the items on a twenty item list, we may be absolutely terrible in the gym. Our body moves so clunkily, the cadence of our workout accelerates and bogs down, we are grunting and not breathing, and tensing instead of relaxing. This generates a whole lot of sweat and injury for a comparatively bad workout. This could be for any myriad of reasons, including experience going to the gym, and pre-knowledge of proper form. It is not that we are naturally bereft in physical intelligence, but it most often means that we are not yet practiced enough at it yet.

Our brain-bodies are always changing relative to the environment, what we do, how we feel about it all, and even how we perceive others perceive us. The poor workout could be because we spend our workdays as an analyst sitting at a desk all day, that our brain-body is primed for sitting and calculating, and not yet accustomed to high activity and gracefully actuating the body in an athletic manner. This requires an entirely different skill set within the brain-body-system, and this all changes through repetitive experience or willful practice over a lifetime, continually, no matter what the task.

Cognition is the wiring arrangement of many trillions of thin and thicker wires from certain sense organs like the eyes, nose, ears, tongue, skin, and internal organs or bodily muscles into the brain and back again. It is also the wiring between certain processing areas within the brain, and the wiring leading out from the action centers of the brain to move the extremities or express ourselves in ways like talking or dancing. It is not only the blueprint, but also what capacity the blueprint allows for. Is it a large volume water tank and electric pumping system, or a small, passive rain-water collection tank? Both have advantageous places and purposes.

Cognition is our evolved mental muscle, or ability potential, at each "gear" within our brain-bodies. Cognition is both the geared engine and the performance that that system can output at any given time, at any given task, in our constant moment-by-moment evolution as a human thinking-engine. The shape of the engine and its performance parameters are the basis of cognition. Mentation, on the other hand, is about what strategies we employ to get the most out of our engine, rest it when needed, or our strategies to use our cognitive engine in innovative ways to solve perplexing, specialized, or generalized problems. Where cognition is *what* one is using, mentation is *how* one uses it.

MENTATION

Mentation is very simply often referred to as "thinking" or "mental activity." This is wildly misleading and this will not be the definition used in this book. Oversimplified terms like "thinking" and "mental activity" are most likely used because for as complex as both cognition and mentation are, mentation may be considered even more *broadly* complex and relativistic. It is difficult to sum up in as many words. "Why do people behave the way they do?" "Why do they think that way?" "Why won't people just do like they are supposed to?" All of these things are the gestalt result of cognition hardware and mentation software's interaction.

The mere act of "thinking" is a product of a variety of interoperating mechanisms and predispositions, as we are beginning to see. It involves innumerable variables over a lifetime and in the moment. A great example we can use to describe mentation, or "mentation style," and how it interlocks with cognition, is the pop-psychology idea of "left and right brainers." Although not a true scientific theory, it is useful as a simplistic diagram of what mentation is.

As it goes, the left-brain / right-brain theory claims that left-brainers see things from a more micro, writing pen perspective, a specialist approach that lends itself to math and logic. Right-brained individuals see the world in a more macro, wide-brush perspective that lends to the language and the arts, or a generalist mode of thinking. However, the actual science on this theory states that this is an oversimplification because we never use just one side of our brain, but the whole brain at once, in varying degrees and balances that are constantly changing relative to environments internal and external.

Seen from this perspective, all of us have a mention style that falls on a spectrum, a complex, constantly changing spectrum; a matrix of an individual mix of left or right-brained, specialist and generalist approaches, changing moment to moment, with left-brainers writing poetry and right-brainers that are analyzing mathematics. All these thinking tools, palates, canvases, and graph papers are being used at the split-second discretion of the individual relative to the available information, the environment originating this information, the pragmatic need to process this information for a specific end-goal, and much, much, more. Mentation is indeed complex, and often confused with cognition as the two overlap in a multitude of areas.

The processes of cognition and mentation work in tandem across the channels of the human thought process; the input channel, or our collection of information from the environment; the throughput channel, our thinking about or processing the information gathered through our senses and from the environment; and finally the output channel, how we conclude or act based on the information flow. The channels are of both our cognition and mentation, and the mention would be *how*, *in which way*, we utilize these channels in various feedback-loops for an end goal.

Opposed to cognition, or how we process information at a mechanical level, mentation is the way in which we experience, think about, and produce actions based on available information from evolving information processing systems. Again, mentation influences cognition and cognition influences mentation. Both overlap and feed in on one another constantly in real-time. Now, let's move to a brief overview of some more technical, molecular and biological science.

GENETICS AND EPIGENETICS

Our genetics, or our DNA (deoxyribonucleic acid,) is that genetic code which is more or less unchanging throughout our life and defines *what* we are, and also how we think. It is our basic, original blueprint that stays relatively steadfast through our years of constant evolution throughout our lives. Our more actively changing *epi*genetics (markers on DNA, and changes to DNA structures by copying and omitting genes;) changes in response to our life experience and largely influences our view of reality on a shorter time frame. This is how we literally pass our life experiences to our offspring!

Comparatively, epigenetics change a lot, and core DNA changes less.

Our base genetics and evolving epigenetics both largely delineate the framework, or make detailed changes to that framework consistently throughout life, and moment to moment. Both are the blueprint for the density and locations of all sensory and neurotransmission neurons of our central and peripheral nervous systems; our brains, our body's skin, the way our eyes are built, the way our inner ear is shaped, the sensitivity of our smell, and well, virtually everything about us. The very structure of our individual bodies at the genetic level affect experiences of the same events in completely different ways for each individual.

Our epigenetics play a more active role in the shaping of these systems over our lifetimes in response to repeated stimuli from the environment and the way we perceive these events, again in a feedback loop continuing from pre-birth to post-mortem. The human mind-brain-body is indeed a finely tuned, infinitely varied machine that changes continually, much like a *bonsai* tree wrapped around a pole and winding and twisting in response to the weather. We can now see what a foolish task it would be to ask a *bonsai* tree to be "normal," to stand up straight as the more numerous redwood trees.

CONSTANTLY EVOLVING DIVERSE HUMANS

We can now find our way easier to the higher-thinking, higher-road of magnanimous compassion and informed tolerance from the knowledge that we are *all* beautifully diverse, inside and out. Through knowing just how complicated being human is, we can counterintuitively process our perceived differences and questions of others more *accurately*. We can do so with cerebral mindfulness instead of snap, emotional reactions based on guesses and comparisons to "normal." We are *not* the same. Even if we vehemently disagree, this information alone serves as a mitigation strategy that will buy us time to formulate a better response so that we don't accidentally vilify others, or unwittingly vilify *ourselves* in the eyes of others. By understanding that we *never* have the precise, same take on things, we can let ourselves and others off the hook, and find other, better ways of interacting with one another.

We have explored the dynamically evolving systems of cognition and mentation, and how these are influenced by our daily experience and genetic code. We can see that it is unreasonable to expect others to always see it the same way that we do, because it is so obvious to us. We can also see how thinking in terms of "all of us are divergent," is factual. That, "I am neurodivergent, they are neurotypical," "I am normal, they are abnormal," are both inherently stigmatizing, divisive dichotomies. In the beginning of the writing of this book, I came to see the "neurodivergent" / "neurotypical" dichotomy as just another fashionable way to market mental health care and medications, and nothing more. Now, let's take a look at some common pitfalls to human thinking that all of us are guilty of at one time or another.

3

FALLACIES THAT HINDER US

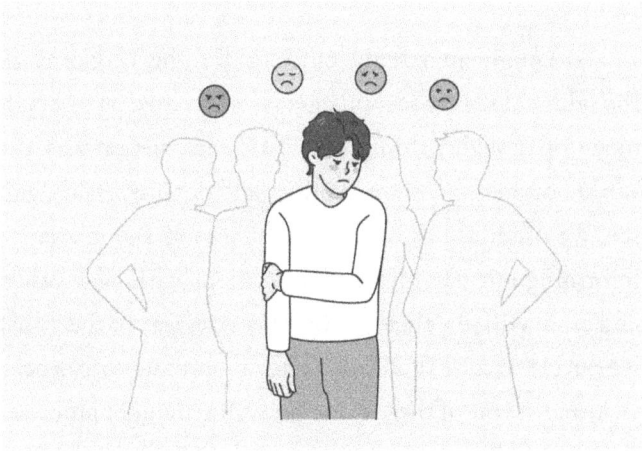

"Us"-thinking requires that we include others into our ideas and conversations. Knowing that humans are diverse by default is the first step to achieving this. The human mind is simply astounding in its complexity and ability for healing and change, but if it is programmed incorrectly, the results can be hurtful and disastrous. Although useful in many situations, certain ways that we process and relay information can be errors in our thinking, or fallacies. These ways of thinking are often used in our media for precisely the reason of speed and efficiency of communication. They make the information easier to convey and digest quickly, and owing to lessened mental effort, they make them more convincing as well. It is here that we need to start drawing a line between how we consume the media and how we transmit this information to one another, or how we think of one another because of the influence of this information.

Although amazingly efficient for the economy of thought and saving mental energy, when used as a default mode of thought, things get lost in translation and the world becomes *more* bewildering, and not less. As we will see, we often use these same strategies as the media for informing our day to day conversations with each other, and as we will see, there are better strategies out there that we can use to solve problems and communicate with others. Below are some of these disempowering thought processes that are causing much of our day to day grief between each other, and act as barriers to fixing our societal ills. Then we will see some proposed solutions for each, straight out of talk therapy, to help us change our own self-imposed suffering, within ourselves and with others.

DICHOTOMOUS (BINARY) THINKING

If normalism is the enemy of how we frame things, dichotomy is the enemy of how we understand and decide things. We have an evolved inclination for dichotomous, or "black and white thinking." It is also known as "binary thinking." Humans have a compulsion to judge things as either "good" or "bad," many times leaving no room in between. Most of us resort to this as our main mode of judgment, unless we are first taught to recognize that this can be a pitfall to more accurate judgment. We do this because it takes less mental effort to split a judgment in a binary fashion, two ways, than it does to engage in spectral thinking, that is, thinking about things as being on a spectrum, more of which we will read about in a moment.

Because of this naturally evolved propensity towards dichotomous thinking that is further conditioned into us en masse, by our wide-spread over-consumption of media that uses dichotomies to keep explanations sweet and simple, and make points more rapidly convincing; we have become harshly judgmental to a degree that is unhealthy. We have a myriad of common dichotomies that we use to get our heads around complex or abstract concepts. "Normal or *ab*normal," "healthy or diseased," and "brain or body," are just some examples of the many ultimately misleading, somewhat *false* dichotomies that we often use.

These dichotomies can be truisms, but somehow are counterproductive and lend to more confusion and misinformation than understanding. Good and relevant scientific examples of flawed, though *partially* true dichotomies are "healthy or diseased," and "brain or body." It is a fallacy to think that we are consistently healthy and then *suddenly* become sickened, and "diseased." The truth is, unless we are talking about things like broken bones, we most often *evolve* into a diseased state over time, sometimes years, as in a sugar-heavy diet induced Type-2 diabetes from consuming too much sugar, too often, and for too *long*. Cirrhosis of the liver from drinking too much alcohol, too often, and for too *long*.

Next, let's look at "brain and body." It is another bedside woe of doctors that we view our brains and other body parts as somehow separate from our bodies. The truth is our brain is, yes, an organ within our bodies, but it *is* our body, as our bodies *contain* our brain. The body is more accurately conceived as a complete unit that does not have "parts" like a washing machine or a car. This incorrect conceptualization and separation of the brain, internal organs, bones, muscles and skin lead us to the misinformed idea that when we get sick, that the sickness is confined to, or "caused" by certain areas of our body. This is false, as any disease anywhere in the body is either contributing to the sickness, or affecting some other part of the body in some way. Even in the case of a sudden broken bone, it can cause inflammation of the surrounding muscle and even puncture the skin. This can cause infection that can spread all throughout the body if not treated properly. No part of our body is an island.

In the same way, we misunderstand that exercising our bodies only builds muscles, and we often don't consider that it makes our entire body healthier, including our brain. This perception of disease and exercise due to an oversimplifying dichotomy leads to incorrect perceptions of what it means to be healthy and how to avoid disease. When we get sick, it is our *entire* body, including our brains that are affected as a singular unit. Also when we exercise, not only do the muscles in our arms, abs, and legs improve, but also our heart, brains, stomach, intestines, kidneys, pancreas, etc.; the entire body benefits.

Knowing that exercise is a major mitigating factor for most common diseases within any area of the body, instead of just diseases of the heart for instance, and that exercise can also increase our mental acuity and cognitive performance, make our facial complexion better, and thus literally reverse physical decline in aging, all at once; it would most likely be a much more attractive reason for us to exercise and eat right, rather than simply to build muscle or lose weight.

It must be noted that our seemingly detached mental health also affects our entire body. Mental health is more important to our bodies than we realize, yet we often section it off to simply the thoughts in our head. Consistently relaxed and happy mental states, along with good diet and exercise affect the onset of diseases and the length of our lives dramatically. Cancer is a great example. Becoming cancerous can often be the result from years of poor lifestyle choices, and more rarely, solely as a result of environmental toxins like second-hand smoking alone. Those with poor lifestyle choices, chronic loneliness, *and* exposure to second-hand smoke will have an astronomically higher risk of becoming cancerous.

Someone with a regular healthy diet and exercise regimen, a supportive family and active social life, and the same exposure to second-hand smoke, have *dramatically* lower rates of cancer. The case is also true for those who have a poor lifestyle, *but* are happy, are optimistic, have many social connections, and have the same exposure to second-hand smoke; they tend to remain cancer free. Our mental health can be a defining factor to literally keep us cancer-free even though it is not experienced as a physical part of our body.

As we can see, dichotomies can be incredibly destructive to proper understanding of some critically important concepts to staying alive. The idea of always being healthy, and then suddenly "getting" a disease is thus oversimplified, and so it becomes a misleading, somewhat false dichotomy. Believing in this misconception leads to all kinds of poor lifestyle choices, because we aren't accurately understanding how our body is a singular unit, and why good self-care and mental health are just as much a cause of cancer as second-hand smoke. Other considerations that we make in our judgments are the same; "good" or "evil," "friend" or "foe." Relying on these kinds of dichotomies as our default mechanism for judgment leads to the same kind of dangerous miscalculation, and stubborn tunnel vision in all kinds of important situations.

For as much mental energy as it conserves, thinking in terms of dichotomies is counterproductively and counterintuitively *inefficient*, wasting more energy than conserved due to the stress of miscalculation and consistent frustration in accurately understanding things; and as we have seen it can even be deadly. Dichotomies often precipitate arguments and sustain arguments because of the oversimplified viewpoints that are being argued and the limited number of options available for recourse. Dichotomies cause us to judge too negatively or too positively as anything slightly outside of "good" or "acceptable," is automatically "bad" and "unacceptable;" and anything that isn't "bad," is automatically "good." Dichotomies are a cancer of thought for many of us.

SPECTRAL THINKING

The answer to changing dichotomous thinking is a thought process known as "spectral thinking." When talking to those that have earned a post-grad degree, we may notice a distinct difference in the way that many size up the world compared to most others. This is "spectral thinking." Spectral thinking is higher-game analysis that doesn't fall into the trap of the dichotomous thinking described above. Spectral thinking is like judging on a spectrum of "A, B, C, D, E," (1 to 5 scale,) "best," "good," "bad," "terrible," "absolutely not;" " and not "A or B," (good or bad.) The reason that this is done, let's say by mental health providers, is that nobody gets a diagnosis of attention deficit hyperactivity disorder (ADHD,) and completely loses the ability to focus at all. This is true for all conditions, not only in the case of autism *spectrum* disorder (ASD,) but also lesser used bipolar *spectrum* disorder (BSD,) and even schizophrenia; they all are thought to fall on a spectrum from (do not have, mild, moderate, severe, debilitating.) They are not simply a case of "completely have," and "do not have" a diagnosis.

Another, more pragmatic way to utilize spectral thinking in our daily lives is to use it next time we get into a disagreement with someone, or find someone offensive. At the current rate, most of us are dichotomizing each other in the news and on the road, "ok" and "not ok," "appropriate" or "inappropriate." We forget that we are the ones deciding this, and that not everybody is not as "normal" as we are. This is incredibly destructive to those of us using this dichotomy for several reasons. Once we relegate someone to the "not ok" category, it is very hard to get them back, and if we publicly insult them over it, this person that could have one day been the person to come back and save our lives, never returns. Also, it can make us seem judgemental to others, and make others put us in the "not OK" category because of our "not OK"-ness with too many others. We are then left wondering why we have so few choices for friends. Spectral thinking essentially cuts the amount of those that we dislike, and increases the number in at least the "minimally interesting" friend pool. Spectral thinking is "us"-thinking because it takes diversity into account. Thinking in our own best interest, *and* the best interest of others comprising *us* can be done automatically by incorporating diversity into our thinking.

Spectral thinking isn't only applicable to mental health diagnosis, treatment, and coping with stress, but it is also extremely beneficial for virtually any other judgment that we make in life. Using spectral thinking instead of "good / bad" dichotomies can lead to a better assessment of the quality of the dissatisfaction and ultimately lead to less stress in misunderstanding, less frustration in miscalculation, and less embarrassment from over-reacting in front of others. Spectral thinking helps us retain logic in stressful situations and keeps one stoic. It helps us think before we speak or act. Spectral thinking helps us better get our head around things instead of quickly bashing our heads through them.

Although the news and advertising may feed us dichotomies left and right, it behooves us to sit back and juggle this information back into a spectrum when we think about it and how we apply it to others. For best results, start with applying three-scale judgment to everything; "yes (good,)" "no (bad,)" and, "on the fence (so-so.)" "A, B, C," and then build it over time to "good, bad, so-so, and don't care;" "A, B, C, D," and so forth. Giving ourselves at least one more option other than "good," and "bad," makes all the difference here. The more options, the *better* judge we become.

SINGLE-CAUSE / SINGLE-SOLUTION

It is not only dichotomous thinking, but also "single-cause / single-solution"-thinking, the analysis and approach to problem solving which is born out of the same desire to conserve mental energy; that is problematic as well. When we think in dichotomies, we are conserving mental energy. The same is true while thinking quickly about how to solve a problem or why it occurred. In our effort to conserve mental energy, "single-cause / single-solution" analysis and problem solving unwittingly pigeonholes our judgment by fooling us into believing that all problems are caused by only one, some thing, and that, that one thing naturally only has one solution.

Because of our fast-paced media that uses dichotomies and "single-cause / single-solution"-thinking to make information more bite-sized and easily digestible; our busy culture, stuck in quick response fight or flight mode, produces destructive psychological hiccups in our thinking. Many overseas view Americans as more prone to polarizing arguments and wordings, rash and poor decision making, and even being stigmatizing and discriminatory, even though this is absolutely *not* who we advertise ourselves to be. This is of no genetic fault of our own, but a cultural glitch reinforced by the mode of delivery of information by the media. Viewed enough times day in and day out, we too begin to think in these terms for ourselves in the need to conserve mental energy. We do it to adapt and react quickly, and to be convincing to others when relaying this dichotomized, over-simplified, and thus highly convincing information from the media to others. It becomes even more disconcerting when we realize that we do this to information concerning ourselves and others. This creates misunderstanding and conflict.

"Single-cause / single-solution"-thinking is terribly counterproductive for as much mental energy as it helps us conserve. It helps us get to root causes and fixes much quicker. Yet, oftentimes we will find this to be inaccurate because ultimately, most problems have many causes, there are a given number of solutions, and sometimes a combination of solutions necessary to properly solve a problem once and for all. When we combine "single-cause / single-solution"-thinking with dichotomies, the results can entail a great amount of tunnel vision and be a quick and catastrophic, fast-food-answer, as opposed to a comprehensive, slow-cooked plan to decisive action that ultimately saves time and effort, and fosters serenity concerning any given problem.

MANY CAUSES / MANY OPTIONS

The best way to counteract the terribly limiting and frustrating, "single-cause / single-solution," absolutist, often fatalistic and catastrophizing thinking; is to consider the possibilities and the options. To acknowledge that any problem can be caused by multiple things, that anybody is more than one thing at a time, or that there are usually several reasons for anything; we get a clear picture of the situation. We can see that anything seen as a problem can have a multi-faceted solution, or sometimes that it may take many steps to undo a knot. We can begin to get a clearer, more accurate judgment of the situation, and much more efficient and effective problem solving in the long run.

Most things happen for *many* reasons, not just one, and any given problem usually has a palette of possible solutions. It is when we forget these things that we find we feel anxious or angry towards others, overwhelmed by life, or frustrated that we just can't fix the problem. Learning to be more considerate of multiple circumstances and remembering that we have options can go miles towards being more compassionate and thinking slower. It helps us not jump to the convenient, quick-fix, feel-good, snap-judgements of our egos, and sometimes with an ultimately *self*-destructive temper tantrum.

Interesting to many that post on social media, spectral thinking and "many-causes / many-solutions"-thinking can help us form better arguments. As many of us instinctively resort to judgmental dichotomies and quick and sloppy "single-cause / single-solution" analysis and problem solving when forming an argument, it becomes easier to counter most arguments, or form a better one if we bring up all of the other reasons why something might happen, and all of the other solutions that there would be to solve it. Noting the complex nature of an argument with spectral thinking and "many-causes / many-solutions"-thinking, one can play a great devil's advocate. This also works great for conflict *resolution* as well.

These two techniques, "spectral thinking" and "many causes / many options"-thinking can turn any of us into a leader for the "us" movement, and leader by example; with the mental stamina and serenity necessary to see change through to the end, day after day. This is what the world needs, and this is how easy it can be to begin to make miracles happen.

MELTING-POT TO SALAD-BOWL

Growing up in elementary school before the 1990s, many of us were probably being taught the "melting pot" analogy to describe American life. This model was intended to be a model for inclusivity by pointing out that we all have something to offer the stew, as our individual ingredients melt into our common culture stew. In later years, this began to be construed to mean assimilation into the stew of the ruling white majority. Alarms were raised over this analogy. Some were saying that this was tantamount to saying that all of us must conform to the white majority culture of the times and folkways of the stew. What followed this "melting-pot" analogy was the currently accepted "salad-bowl" analogy that I was recently taught in sociology class.

The salad-bowl analogy is to say that we all have our own individualized ingredients, coexisting together with the romaine lettuce dominating the salad-bowl, in small enclaves here and there. This is correct for the way things are these days, as it is exactly the "we"-thinking that has got us into this toxic salad to start with. This was touted in my college textbook as an evolution over the "melting-pot" model as it allows for all of us to be ourselves. Unfortunately, this model is a *devolution* of the "melting-pot" model on the grounds of "united we stand, divided we fall." It's divisive, and not inclusive at all.

According to the Civil Rights Acts, we may never be discriminated against concerning things like our age, sex, race, color, gender, gender expression, sexual orientation, and mental and marital status among others. Isn't it ironic, even hypocritical in some sense that these are the exact labels actually being utilized in this discriminatory salad-bowl of pride and "inclusivity" (exclusivity) that we see today? Wouldn't our *true* identities, the ingredients that we have to offer others in the salad, more appropriately be that information which supersedes these things? Are we a *kind* person? Are we a hard worker? Are we a team player? Are we good at math? Do we like photography? As stated throughout the book, it is this exclusive "we"-thinking touted as inclusivity that is dividing our country and not uniting it nor making it inclusive. Although it has served to start important conversations, doing away with this now antiquated, exclusive discrimination is common sense. What we actually need is the "us"-thinking, "rainbow-sherbet" model.

RAINBOW SHERBET ICE CREAM

In the last several decades, we have made the move from a "melting-pot" society to what is now commonly referred to in sociology classes in elementary and secondary education as a "salad-bowl" model for society. These are both incorrect distortions of inclusivity that are assimilation and exclusivity respectively. Both are false analogies because they derive from "we"-thinking. One, assimilating to the ruling majority of a particular race, and the other standing out from one another as a *divided*, diversified "we the people;" "we over here, and we over there, and we over here." The "salad-bowl" also makes the same mistake of resting the ingredients over a still homogenized majority. In a *truly* inclusive society, a ruling majority should be composed of *all* of us, "The People," "the mixed-majority," "the rest of all of us." Any "we"-group that is created in the population is always "we" relative to not just the dominant majority, but all other "we"-groups co-existing as well.

The Power of Us proposes to us a "rainbow sherbet" approach as the clear glass of water in this argument. Rainbow sherbet works as an accurate and equitable depiction of how our society should aim to function. Each flavor of the rainbow shines individually within a single scoop of ice cream that contains all colors in a *seamless gradient*. It makes sense because in order for us to have a label, we must first be human to begin with. In this sense, all persuasions are unified as one scoop, consisting of all banners of diversity. It becomes a common, yet nuanced national identity of *all* of our equal choosing.

The "salad-bowl," though an earnest try, considering the proposed assimilation to the ruling white class of the "melting-pot" analogy, is inherently divisive in a deceptively democratic way, and not unifying as advertised. In fact, it could equally be argued that the "salad-bowl" is a step backwards, as now all of the parts are separated from one another and not unified at all. Sure, we can attempt to unify this salad by drizzling on a monolithic dressing of law and economics to force conformity, but in doing so we would essentially be relinquishing our power as a unified "The People" to politicians and industry respectively; their richness detracting from the taste of the individual ingredients of the salad. This is what our "inclusive" salad-bowl is costing us today. Conformity, like assimilation, is not unity.

The salad-bowl is a "we" concept, and not an "us" concept. The "rainbow-sherbet" model is a great example of a higher-game "us" concept that is a true evolution of the melting-pot society *and* the salad-bowl. If we are to find *true* unity, we must opt *not* to stand out proudly from one another, making demands and requests for preferential treatment and accommodation to the mixed-majority. Neither can we find unity by depending on third-party, public institutions or private industry to do it for us. We can only achieve public unity by having all of our flavors present in a single, delicious scoop of ice cream.

In this chapter, we have discussed flaws to human thinking derived from "we"-thinking, the damage caused, and some proposed "us"-thinking solutions to these maladaptive thinking patterns, so that we can then help others through our compassion by all of us belonging to the same group. By implementing any one of these techniques, any one of us can take affirmative steps toward the realization of a kinder, more accessible, *human* society for all. Whether neurotypical, latino, female, black, Gen Z, neurodivergent, white, elderly, gay, asian, transexual, married, multi-race, divorced, vegan, or meat-lover, we *can* have a society that is for all of us. Can we all agree that this is a lot of exclusive labels of protected classes? This, except for dietary preference of course...

SECTION

4

PROJECTS FOR US TO MAKE CHANGE

Now that we've made some minor adjustments in order to make the jump to "us" a little less strenuous, here are some projects that need urgent fulfillment in society in order to make it a better place for all. Each one is only a brief description and are seeds of ideas that I hope will inspire us to think outside of the box on these otherwise perplexing issues, using the power of "us"-thinking. We will go in the usual order of poverty and greed, bullying, drug use, mental health, homelessness, and mass incarcerations. We will conclude with a recap on how these changes will positively affect our collective quality of life.

All of the ideas listed below were thought up in late fall of 2022 when I myself had been impacted by a large number of these social conditions at once. The trauma and stress within myself stemming from multiple, compounding discriminations and stigmas had reached such a boiling point that I spent an entire month manically thinking and writing about these problems, secluded in rental housing that I was able to scrape enough money to sit in and heal for a while. It was during this period of immense psychological torment that I feel that I came up with some of the best ideas of my life, and I sincerely hope that you will agree. Even if only one or two of these seeds of ideas seem like a good idea, please take a moment at the end to imagine just how much better off the world would be if we implemented them. These visions have been a big inspiration for the writing of this book, and it is a dream that I find delight in for myself having dared to dream it in the first place. Let's get started.

PLAN #1 A BETTER ECONOMICS

"Us" economics. Greed in America has been gaining attention in recent years. It is widely accepted that this problem is impossible to solve as well, and that any change will bring with it a substantial loss to our economy. Ideas have been floated on how to tackle the problem, but most have failed. I often wonder why we need to change anything, because if something works, but isn't producing a favorable result, we can change how we use it, without attempting to fix an already working system. The following "us"-idea for better economics aims to be a retrofit, be a firmware update to our current system and not a replacement for it. This proposed upgrade is simple and consists of a reinterpretation of the words of Adam Smith, the father of our modern economics.

"Individual interest serves the common good."

This fundamental quote seems to have been misinterpreted to mean, "Every man for himself~!" It appears to have become a reason for a self-centered cash-grab that totally disregards public health. What we seem to have missed is the *"common"* part. This quote would be more authentically translated as, "We must take care of ourselves, before we can take care of others. Or, "we take care of ourselves so that we *can* take care of others." This quote can easily be translated any of these three ways, and the latter two are obviously more preferable. They are preferable because as a leading nation on the world stage, one would expect that we are choosing the finest strategy to make our money, feed and house our population, and fuel innovation.

The way that this new interpretation of Adam Smith is the best solution is that it is "us"-thinking economics and not "we"-thinking economics. We have already seen the fallacy in the idea of "we" and how inherently exclusionary it is. Is it then no wonder why our current economic theory based on this "we"-mentality is exclusionary to a larger number of us than the few of us in the in-group? When we change this economic theory from the "we" of "you and I get rich," to the "us" of "you" and "I" and "they," *all* get rich, then something glaringly obvious, yet miraculous happens. We *all* get richer. It creates an upward spiral and not a trickle-down.

There are many ways that we could seek to make our economics an "us"-economics. One such way is to popularize ownership of corporations above what we have done in the past. It is similar to the communist idea of government-owned corporations, but it is not the government doing the ownership, but the public. This may have been the original intent of our economics before it was shaped to only be owned by a small portion of the public. Strategies like sectioning shares smaller so that investment is more affordable to those with lower income, or selling company stock in-store to make it convenient for consumers to become owners comes to mind. At the current, inaccessibility due to start-up investment cost, inconvenience, and overcomplification of the system are major factors why more of us do not own more stock, and why the population has such little control over corporations. We need to design our economics with the ease-of-use of a smartphone so that *all* can participate.

Some of the benefits that could be expected may include:

- Less need for government regulation and oversight, owing to the increased, direct influence of the consumer over corporations.

- More direct power for consumers concerning what corporations are selling to us.

- More operating capital for corporations.

If we are committed to keep our foothold on the world stage as its forerunning leader in cultural and economic innovation and we are working to be the pinnacle, top-dog in the world economy; would it then not compel us to take the strategy producing the *best* result and not the second best result? Thinking about not just oneself, but the group as well is what generates the best result. Making everyone owners in a convenient way to drive up trading volume, would stop class warfare and greed between owners and consumers, and it would stop the greed creating paradigm of leaving others out. Profit for a few, or profit for all? We need to start asking ourselves the question, "What is capital?"

PLAN #2 STOP BULLYING

If there is no greater affront to "us"-thinking; it is bullying. In this late fall of 2022 mentioned earlier, I had a vision while sitting on a city bus that would change my life forever. I envisioned an "economy of suffering," passed on using bullying as a transmission medium, that was jumping from person to person. I began to notice how we will bully each other in customer service interactions. For instance, I would go to the doctor and tell them that I had an appointment, expecting to be checked in and seated. I was then sternly asked, "did you call to confirm the appointment," as a formality, but in an overly-curt tone of voice. I thought, "why is this relevant?" The receptionist rolled her eyes, and said, "well, next time, be sure to confirm the appointment," as if she was deeming me kosher to have my appointment by patronizing me on my adherence to their policy that I knew nothing about prior. It wasn't so much what was being said, but the way it was said. Instead of being informative, it was patronizing and fault-finding. It was also the beginning of my noticing how some don't answer requests for service, but question them instead.

I began to notice this everywhere. I started to notice that whenever I would ask a receptionist, customer care representative, or bus driver a question, that they would question my asking the question before they would try to simply answer my question or be of service to my request.

Instead of answering a question or request, others would question the question, making things only more difficult and slowing down business, frustrating both me and themselves. I began to see this meaningless and superior behavior as a conditioned, defensive stance to bullying in their own lives. We are often feeling bullied at work, feeling used in our service to others, and not valued and treated equally. I thought to myself, "Who wouldn't be aloof, moody, and antagonistic?"

It was mortifying to see the world in this way. I have since begun to see this everywhere else, people yelling, horns honking, dogs barking. I see it so much to the point that it has become a commonplace expectation of mine to expect a rebuke or a criticism for virtually everything that I ask for in a customer service interaction. Sometimes it doesn't happen, and God bless those that don't bring their hurt to work, but it does happen way too often regardless. Many opt to blame, shame, and criticize each other before being of service to others. They feel that they are owed more. Customers feel they are entitled too much. I noticed this with particular frequency in the city. It is now a deep-seated conviction of mine that we in fact, live in a truly "bully society" that is fueled by normalism.

Our entire social currency has become problem-oriented and one-upping. Gripes and complaints, criticisms, and cynicism dominate the subject of our conversations. Do we ever have anything positive or encouraging to say? As if we are all watching the news all day long, we are consistently focused on what is *wrong*. Not, "how can I help," or "what a beautiful day." We seem to think that the best way for us to help anybody with their service issue is to point out what is wrong with them for needing the service in the first place. I think it is apparent to anybody who has driven a car in the last thirty years that bullying is a social currency for far too many. We honk at each other with over one-hundred feet of space between us, and sometimes just flat out flip each other off for not being in the right lane. We feel against the world or that the world is out to get us. It is everywhere, it is out of control, it is senseless, and we, *the adults*, must be the ones to stop it. Hurt people hurt people, and this is what our society has become. Too many hurt people with inflamed narcissism.

In order to end bullying as we know it, we must come to the same conclusion on the following issues:

• Bullying is not simply a children's issue. Children model adults, and the adults are teaching children to bully because the children are watching them. We, including the children, watch it on TV, we watch others honking, cutting off each other purposefully, and raging. This becomes "normal." We see our parents bullying each other and talking foul about others, and sometimes we are bullied by family members, hurting the ones we love first. The children are taking this to school, not bringing it home. It is therefore upon *adults* to stop bullying in society.

- Bullying is a side-effect of marketing lofty expectations of the way we look, behave, and the things that they own as an inadvertent side-effect of consumerism and marketing. It stems from a misperception that what we see on TV is "normal," what everyone is doing; when nothing could be further from the truth.

- Violence as entertainment needs to stop and be treated in the same way as vulgar language and sexuality on TV and in the media. It gives us the impression that it is "normal" or even favorable to be aggressive. We are only modeling what we get in the media. The children are only modeling us.

- There ought to be more stiff penalties for road rage and roadway bullying, such as exiting, stopping, or using a vehicle on a public roadway with intent to threaten or harm.

This idea is very simple as it requires virtually no infrastructure to accomplish. It can mostly be done within the confines of the human heart and mind. The major problem to stopping bullying is that we are not yet recognizing it as a society-wide problem affecting *all* of us. Any problem that we identify within children is almost certainly learned behavior. I made up a thought experiment concerning bullying, and that was that we would know that we had defeated bullying in our society when our pets would stop barking so much and being aggressive. Our pets are also only modeling us too. If we weren't so tense, neither would they be.

PLAN #3 BETTER DRUG USE

Anyone that has spent any time addicted to drugs or treating addicts knows that there is more wrong with drugs in America than just The War on Drugs. There are several points for improving the situation, some of which require a better public awareness of addiction, and the other parts require a greater infrastructure to deal with drug use and addiction treatment. First, let's start with a better awareness of what drugs are and what addiction truly is.

Anybody that has had a morning coffee, green tea, or even herbal tea has done drugs; drugs being "any compound that changes the functioning of the brain or the body." If we add sugar to that beverage, then we are guilty of doing drugs twice. Refined sugar easily fits this definition of a drug. Food can change the functioning of our brain-bodies, and so some foods we eat, can essentially be the same as doing drugs if we are ingesting a substance to get a desired effect. *All* things in the material world are made of chemicals. We thus live a chemically dependent reality. Everything from the turkey on the plate on the table in front of the chair that we sit on, the fork we hold, the water we drink, and including our own bodies; are *all* made of chemicals. Chemical puritanism is a conceptual fallacy, and holiness is a matter of faith and is a lifestyle choice.

Addiction is misunderstood in the same way, and just as pervasive. If we are drinking coffee compulsively throughout the day everyday and get a caffeine headache when we stop, then we are an addict as we are having withdrawal symptoms. If we can't stop eating gummies, though we gain weight, then we are also an addict. If we can't stop eating chicken fried steak, despite congestive heart failure, then we are, again, an addict. Too many of us want to believe that just because they don't do street meth or fentanyl that they are not an addict. That they are "normal." Again, going back to "normal," this is a delusion. The plain truth is that *most*, if not *all* of us are addicted to something that causes us some form of negative consequence in some way, yet we keep doing it. This is part of being human, as this is how our reward system functions, not only "an addict's brain," but all of our brains. Alas, we are all addicted to dopamine.

The truth is that drugs and addictions are everywhere. They are in our food, they are in our entertainment. They are in our phones, and even the cars that we drive compulsively to get anywhere lest we soon get cabin fever; finding it difficult to walk anywhere to save our lives. The fact of the matter is that *most* of us are using drugs, have an addiction, or are dependent on something of some kind. An addiction doesn't only happen when one uses illicit drugs or junk food, but often involves prescribed or over-the-counter drugs. Promiscuity and porn, impulse shopping, gambling, over eating, and screen time on our devices are other things that can cause negative consequences, yet we do them anyway.

For us to be looking down on others as "addicts," we would be both ignorant and a hypocrite, *and* delusional too. Addicts *are* us. What we need is help to realize what we have gotten ourselves into, and often when we find good help, we end up better off than others. It is only until we reach this fair illustration of what drugs and addiction are that we can seek help for ourselves and seek to help others without being patronizing and religious. As well as a spiritual problem, it is a biological one, and also a question of identity. Below are some ideas for a new legalization effort for drugs that includes proper drug use and rehabilitation treatment:

LEGALIZATION

We need to legalize single use quantities of drugs, as many other countries are already starting to do with fabulous results. Drugs are chemistry and available in nature, and unfortunately, drugs are never going away. We will only waste our time, money, and resources continuing to "combat the problem" instead of accepting reality. By accepting reality, it has been proven the world over in countries like Portugal, that, with the right infrastructure, legalizing drugs actually leads to a *decrease* in drug use, not more of it.

BETTER DRUGS

One of the major problems with drugs in the United States is the poor quality of drugs on the street. Often adulterated with other compounds owing from shotty clandestine manufacture, drugs on our streets are more dangerous than just the drug alone. By legalizing drugs, drugs can be put under the supervision of the Food and Drug Administration (FDA,) and this would require that drugs sold in the US be of a United States Pharmacopeia (USP,) grade purity. Having access to drugs as they are advertised to start with is the second step to combating the deadly aspect of the drug epidemic that we currently see today.

BETTER DOSING

Most users of any drug generally have no idea about the proper dosing required to get the desired effects from the drugs with the least amount of side effects. The good news is that this information is available in common medical pharmacology. By having proper education into harm reduction methods of responsible and proper drug use, users can then begin to take reasonable quantities of drugs. With the more tame and predictable drug use that this would create, there would be a sharp decline in drug related 911 calls for overdoses and abnormal behavior. Most that are using drugs are currently eyeballing doses of unreliable substances of unknown purity, and this is contributing to the problems associated with drug use, much more than the presence of the drugs themselves.

ADMINISTERED BY PHARMACIST

A crucial aspect to keeping legalization from becoming a free-for-all for both users and organized crime is the birth of a licensed pharmacist-run, drug pharmacy / dispensary. Drugs would be sold in limited supplies of single use doses by licensed pharmacists who would be able to offer educated advice on how to use the drug without ruining one's good time, the safety of others, or the life of the user. It is about enjoying our drugs and to stop this practice of poisoning ourselves with them. Some of the most destructive drugs available of all drugs are currently available at corner stores across the country, and so it is not radical to ask that less harmful drugs also be available.

BETTER DRUG TREATMENT

I have had addiction issues of my own in the past, and when I went to seek help, I far too often found the services patronizing and ineffective. One way, I would be handed a Bible, and in the other direction, others would tell me their therapy was "evidenced-based," but was basically the same stigmatizing and patronizing, shaming and fault-finding dogma of the religious approach dressed as science. Normalist society is simply forcing conformity to "normal." Drug addiction *is*, in fact, a spiritual issue; an issue of seeing too little beauty in the world. Yet, this spiritual deficit is most often caused by trauma involving love and belonging, and personal identity as well.

We must administer addiction treatment programs on a bio-psycho-social-spiritual model to see the best results. As was the case with myself, and virtually all other addicts I have met, drug use is a convenient way to escape an unsatisfying life. It is an earnest attempt to colorize a life that feels drab, black and white, or lonely. This is why finding God does work. But not only must we find a spirituality that works for us, but we must also work to find others to share a beautiful life with. We must, most importantly, work to find *ourselves* in order to be able to define what a beautiful life is to us to begin with. After all of this has been accomplished, we must also learn to take care of ourselves. This is a tall order and can take a tremendous amount of reckoning, courage, and self-discovery, and so this process is best facilitated by counseling professionals, not a normalist, fault-finding, or religious dogma alone. *This* kind of model will revolutionize addiction treatment with the power of "us"-thinking.

All of these combined efforts, along with an updated and medically approved awareness of what drugs are and what addiction is would go far in ameliorating much of the social stigma concerning drugs. Then drug use could be a choice; favorable to some, unacknowledged by others, and even despised by others in this free America, where we have the right to make our own decisions as mature and consenting adults. We would no longer be going down dark alleyways to get our drugs, organized crime would no longer be selling the drugs, police would then be able to focus on more pressing matters like violent crime that are currently exacerbated by our putting drugs in the closet to start with. We would be able to easily spot suspiciously high people in the neighborhood and offer to walk them home, as opposed to calling the police and catastrophizing the situation in xenophobia and excessive fear.

All in all, implementing these changes to our War on Drugs would effectively end The War on Drugs, and would bring safety to our communities. They would bring the end-goal without the struggle, by changing it to an "us"-issue instead of "we against them"-issue. The War on Drugs has been a *disaster*, and we will never win unless we do away with chemistry, which is practically impossible.

Even in the case of this impossibility, where there be a will be a way. Some would find a way to continue making them, only at an increased detriment to public and personal health. Sometimes the best way to win is to stop fighting.

PLAN #4 A BETTER MENTAL HEALTH

For almost 175 years since the advent of modern psychiatry in the 1850s, we have been practicing a pathologizing model of mental health. Since the dawn of wide-spread chemical, pharmaceutical treatments in the 1950s, and up to the present day, we have increasingly become dependent on medication alone to treat our mental health conditions. This specialized and pathologizing, purely scientific approach, for all of its studies and formulas, has made mental healthcare anything but mentally healthy.

A newer holistic approach has become increasingly popular over the last couple of decades. Though unfortunately it is still not the norm, and medication-only, profit-centric doctors still outnumber holistic-healing, patient-centric ones; it behooves us to continue moving in this direction. Yet, as encouraging as the development of holistic psychiatry is, there is still a problem lurking in both of these systems, and this is the practice of pathologizing the patient as a means of treatment.

Psychiatrists of both genres predominantly look at what is *wrong* with us, and not what is *good* about us. We are asking only what is wrong, what needs to be hammered down or numbed out, rather than what is right, and what needs to be propped up, polished, or mastered. We are still pathologizing as a mental health practice instead of playing to our strengths. Using positive psychology to enhance what is good about our cognitive hardware and mentation software is better than finding what's wrong about it, and just squashing it down with heavy medication in an attempt to escape from ourselves.

It is time for a new mental health. Below is a plan to improve on the existing system under a rather ambitious, model institution I dub a "self-mastery center," (SMC.)

Imagine a doctor's office, a psychiatrist's office, and a counseling and case management office all rolled into one. This is the vision of a new kind of psychiatry, an SMC. At these facilities, anybody, not just those that are afraid that they have a mental illness, but anybody looking for a higher standard of living can get access to all manner of self-improvement tools and strategies; much like a gym for the mind with trainers. The center would employ personnel that specialize in the below mentioned skills and counseling:

HOLISTIC VS. SPECIALIZED MENTAL HEALTHCARE

These SMC centers would be focused on the holistic health of the client, different from the medication-centric mental health practice that we see today. It has been long established that medication alone is not the best solution to treating mental health conditions. When talk-therapy is combined with medication, and behavioral and lifestyle modification therapies, outcomes are bar none, much more favorable and sustainable than the over-specialized, medication-for-diagnosis model that is in widespread use today. In fact, medication-only therapies often are found to *worsen* patient outcomes because psychiatric conditions are not treated like aspirin for headache as expected. Psychiatric medications help, but they do not erase symptoms. They only help *a little*.

SELF-DISCOVERY THERAPY (SDT)

An SMC would facilitate enhancement of the client's holistic physical, mental, social, spiritual, financial, motivational health, and it would also help the client to identify who they really are. In our current model of mental healthcare, we help the client to understand who the client is *not*, and not who the client *is*. SDT would be a two-pronged approach to this disparity by focusing equally on both; who one is, as well as who one is not. Knowing oneself is arguably one of the most difficult and essential lifetime tasks to living a better life. By facilitating this discovery instead of obscuring it with pathology, the client is freed from self-stigma and subsequent stunted growth from being turned in on, and fearful of themselves and their symptoms. Others will be more accepting of us too, because of who we are, and not what diagnosis we have.

LIFE COACHING COUNSELING

Along with the positive psychology approach of self-mastery instead of a self-suppression model powered by pathology, an SMC would employ life-coaching services to clients as well. At an SMC, the practitioner or life-coach would not only ask the question, "what is my client suffering from," but also, "who does my client aim to be," and, "how do we get them there?" All too often, clients at mental health clinics feel underserviced because there is an expectation of life skills and motivational training, rather than simply medications and advice to *cope* with their symptoms. After all, we go to therapy because we aren't thriving, not because we aren't coping well enough. We need to change the focus.

LIFE SKILLS CONSULTATION FOR SUSTAINABLE OVERALL HEALTH

An SMC would not only offer psychotherapy, medication, self-discovery, and self-actuation counseling; but also all of the life skills necessary to maintain the new found, healthier and motivated self. Services such as help with personal hobby acquisition, social life skills, cooking and diet education, but also financial health counseling would be available. These extra benefits ensure that the client doesn't run into frustration about life circumstances even though they have found relief from their symptoms and a clear path forward in their new self-knowledge. At these facilities one can access:

- Talk, medication, and behavioral modification therapy by a licensed psychiatrist.

- Counseling for self-discovery and self-mastery, either as a component of talk-therapy with a psychiatrist, or by a certified counselor.

- Life-coaching sessions to keep clients focused, organized, and motivated by a dedicated life-coach.

- Holistic lifestyle modification training that includes: Cooking skills and diet, exercise education, instruction for good sleeping habits.

- Social skills training that includes finding a satisfying personal hobby and maintaining an active social life with healthy relationships.

- Financial skills training and consultation from a licensed professional such as a certified public accountant, (CPA.)

- Personalized holistic, spiritual counseling drawing from the world's major belief systems and practices of the client's choice.

SMCs are a new model for a better, mentally healthy, mental health that does not pathologize the client, but empowers them while also treating their suffering. The SMC could open up a new chapter in our treatment of mental health and close the door on simply disempowering ourselves with mental *sickness*. It would make going to mental health services a thing to be proud of, a place to empower one's dream to be realized, and not an embarrassing place where one only goes if they have problems. It is a model of a more sustainable and preventative mental healthcare that is focused on thriving instead of surviving.

PLAN #5 PROJECT: HOTEL CALIFORNIA

Project: Hotel California (PHC,) is an idea that I birthed in that fall of 2022 in California to help end the homeless crisis. It does so simply by changing our thinking about what homelessness is. It is based on the question, "Why does homelessness need to be a bad thing?" Problems are only problems if they are seen as problems, and not opportunities. PHC seeks to change homelessness from a place of strife, hopelessness, and loneliness, to rehabilitation, hope, and even comradery. The concept originated as a proposition to change an orphaned county jail into a place that sets us free instead of locking us up. We are *all* vulnerable to homelessness, and it behooves us to frame the issue as an "us" issue.

This plan can either be at a central jail facility or a decentralized network of community organizations providing the following concentrated model of service (jail model described):

- Immediate housing support as empty jail cells.

- Daily meals served out of the jail kitchen, eaten in the dayroom.

- Foodstuff purchasable through the jail commissary.

- Showers in the pre-existing shower stalls.

- Television, charging stations, and internet access in the dayroom.

- Laundry available in the jail laundry.

- Centralized counseling and case management services in the facility.

- Drug addiction treatment in the dayroom and medical facility.

- Medical and psychiatric care in the jail medical facility.

- Victim flight support for those fleeing abusive relationships and dangerous situations.

- Permanent housing search support counseling.

- Financial support counseling, stipends, and zero interest micro-loans.

- In-house security and monitoring on location.

In the instance of the jail-based model shown above, all of these services can be provided in-house. This means that clients and providers no longer need to travel back and forth to see each other, making the jobs and lives of the client, case managers, clinicians, housing support, and kitchen volunteers much more efficient and stress free, with lower overall cost in money and time. PHC seeks to make homelessness as we know it today a thing of the past. PHC seeks to turn a desperate, slow downward spiral out of society, into a rapidly uplifting experience and welcoming hand back. The ultimate vision of PHC is that it will be as common as an emergency room (ER.) It can be a life-support service for any of us to get emergency help for any life and livelihood-threatening crisis *outside* of the body.

PHC is a plan to keep us from being incarcerated or unsheltered, and/or unfed on the streets, vulnerable to drug abuse in the first place. We go to PHC before we go to jail, before we become homeless, but for a good reason and in good spirit. The newer systems of going out to the client with services, however innovative and well intentioned, are inherently inefficient and consume much time and resources above what PHC offers. PHC offers a place of refuge where anybody with any non-medical, yet life and livelihood-threatening conditions can go to seek help for themselves. PHC seeks to offer a reframing of "homelessness" from a dead-end street, to a highway back into happy living and society, accessible by *all*.

All of the problems we have discussed here lead into the stain of mass incarceration of the public. All of the areas we named throughout this book all lead to higher crime, arrest rates, and subsequent gun violence. The best way for us to be ameliorating mass incarceration is by working on these other areas individually, and mass incarceration will inevitably follow. Perhaps mass incarceration is the last block in the *kujenga* puzzle of social sickness. As is the case with all of these social ills, the easiest way for us to win these battles is not to fight them in the first place.

RECAP

As we have seen, "us"-thinking could be the keystone that we must move in order to retrofit our capitalist economics positively, but also help to remedy the "unsolvable" greed problem. We have seen that it just doesn't stop here and can play a role in solving an entire host of societal crises we are experiencing; bullying, drug abuse, mental health, homelessness, and mass incarceration. We have seen that all of these problems are not separate, isolated phenomena. We see that we need to deal with the holistic problem. We see the mechanisms of all of the aforementioned crises as interconnected; a syndrome of ills in our society, all proliferating in overlapping feedback loops. We now know the good news is that if we impact any one of the problems in the spirit of "us"-thinking, we will not only impact the target problem, but also all of our other problems that are reciprocally interconnected to a similar degree.

In this book we have:

- Described the fallacy of "we"-thinking and how a shift to "us"-thinking will lead to immeasurable benefits in a multitude of areas currently deemed "impossible" to solve.

- Considered what is wrong with thinking in terms of "normal" and how a shift to a new paradigm of divergency as a culture can be used to undo the logical fallacy of normalism.

- Explored the depths of human consciousness and saw that human thinking is anything but "normal" or "typical," and that each of us is extraordinary in our own right and seek to feel that we are "normal" and competent enough to never be considered "crazy"or objectively "wrong" by anybody.

- Identified some common pitfalls to evolved human thinking in this modern age and offered up "us"-thinking remedies to these pitfalls.

- Read about proposed out-of-the-box solutions to common social ills based on "us"-thinking paradigms that otherwise have been thought of as "impossible to solve."

- Learned that by framing our social problems in terms of "us," by keeping ourselves *and* others in the equation as well, that the entire focus point of these problems change, making them easier to solve, and adding the extra motivation necessary to solve them with urgent effort.

Although this book is simply a general overview of the problems, it is my hope as the author to have this short work serve as an inspiration, a launchpad, or a catalyst for other works to be published and further research to be made on each of these issues individually. It has been a short, yet powerful work that is information dense and packed with a spirit that I hope that you, the reader, have found infectious, hopeful, and new. At the very least, it is my sincere hope that it has opened our eyes to the possibilities for just how simple these problems could be to solve, and in the interest of a *better* America. A better America where we reestablish ourselves as a world leader in not just the economy, but culture, and innovation as well.

FINAL WORD AND ACKNOWLEDGEMENT

I hope you enjoyed reading *The Power of Us*. This has been my first book, and it has definitely been a journey to remember for me, hopefully it was for you as well. I wanted to make this book as information dense as possible because there is nothing more that I dislike than a long book that essentially over-explains things that I already knew. Honestly, at its peak, the book was over 80,000 words and 289 pages long in standard essay format. It is now finished at 18,000 words. I am a little bittersweet over this, but I plan to write many books in the future, each one being better, and probably longer, than the last. Thank you and stay tuned!

I would like to give thanks to my mother for helping me over the years, always sticking by me and supporting me, much to her own self-sacrifice. I would like to thank the numerous friends that have supported me throughout the years and the many friends that I have made all over the globe. I would like to thank a handful of earth angels, truly selfless and powerful, good people, who have helped me along the way. I would like to thank my publisher Milton and Hugo for giving me the opportunity to start my career as a writer, and have been very attentive and accommodating to me. Lastly, I would like to thank God for blessing me, making me who I am, guiding me, protecting me, and keeping me strong through some really tough times.

God bless us all, and thank you for reading.
Joshua David

CITATIONS AND REFERENCE

[1]

Personal income in the United States
https://en.wikipedia.org/wiki/Personal_income
_in_the_United_States

[2]

Facts About Bullying
Assistant Secretary for Public Affairs (ASPA)
https://www.stopbullying.gov/resources/facts

[3]

U.S. Population Growth Rate 1950-2022
https://info.nicic.gov/ces/domestic/population-
demographics/us-population-growth-rate-1950-
2022#:~:text=The%20current%20population%20
of%20U.S.,a%200.49%25%20increase%20from%20
2019.

[4]

Mental Illness
https://www.nimh.nih.gov/health/statistics/mental-
illness

[5]

SAMHSA Announces National Survey on Drug Use
and Health (NSDUH) Results Detailing Mental
Illness and Substance Use Levels in 2021
Substance Abuse and Mental Health Services
Administration (SAMHSA)
https://www.hhs.gov/about/news/2023/01/04/samhsa-
announces-national-survey-drug-use-health-results-
detailing-mental-illness-substance-use-levels-2021.
html

[6]

New Survey Data Provides Demographic Profile of
Population Experiencing Homelessness Who Lived in
Emergency and Transitional Shelters
Glassman
https://www.census.gov/library/stories/2024/02/
living-in-shelters.html#:~:text=It%20is%20not%20
a%20complete,estimated%20was%20582%2C500%20
in%202022.

[7]

Prisoners in 2022 – Statistical Tables

Author(s) E. Ann Carson

https://bjs.ojp.gov/library/publications/prisoners-2022-statistical-tables#:~:text=It%20also%20provides%20data%20on,from%20yearend%202021%20(1%2C205%2C100).

[8]

Mass Incarceration: The Whole Pie 2024

Wagner

https://www.prisonpolicy.org/reports/pie2024.html

[9]

Suicide Data and Statistics

https://www.cdc.gov/suicide/facts/data.html#:~:text=Suicide%20deaths%2C%20plans%2C%20and%20attempts,adults%20seriously%20thought%20about%20suicide.